THE GOLF PUZZLE BOOK

THE GOLF PUZZLE BOOK

Text by Norman Ferguson

An Hachette UK Company
www.hachette.co.uk

Summersdale Publishers Ltd
Part of Octopus Publishing Group Limited
Carmelite House
50 Victoria Embankment
LONDON
EC4Y 0DZ
UK

www.summersdale.com

Printed and bound in CPI Group (UK) Ltd, Croydon, CR0 4YY

ISBN: 978-1-80007-920-5

Substantial discounts on bulk quantities of Summersdale books are available to corporations, professional associations and other organizations. For details contact general enquiries: telephone: +44 (0) 1243 771107 or email: enquiries@summersdale.com.

DISCLAIMER
All information featured in this book was correct at time of print. The author and publishers cannot accept responsibility for any inaccuracies and apologize in advance for any inadvertent errors in reporting.

THE GOLF PUZZLE BOOK

BRAIN-TEASING PUZZLES, GAMES AND TRIVIA FOR GOLF FANS

summersdale

INTRODUCTION

Golf has been played for centuries and there is no sign of interest in playing or watching the game letting up. Over the years, it has seen many changes but remains essentially the same: trying to get a small ball into a small hole in as few strokes as possible. For millions it is a pastime affording a break from the day-to-day routine; for others it's a frustrating battle against the elements and one's own inadequacies. For many – it's both. And yet when that drive sails beautifully high, long and straight, or that putt finds its way home over the bumpiest of greens, there is no feeling like it.

Trying to negotiate a links course in strong winds and driving rain requires skill, knowledge and a little bit of cunning. *The Golf Puzzle Book* should not present as difficult a challenge, but its mixture of anagrams, crosswords, word searches, riddles and more will test even the most knowledgeable of golf fans. A selection of questions on golfing history and trivia will offer a different kind of test. Surely every golf fanatic knows who the Huckleberry Dillinger is, right?

Please take your time to enjoy the varied puzzles on offer in this book – there are no penalties for slow play!

CROSSWORD

BAD SHOTS

ACROSS

2 It's the bottom (3)
3 You'll be down at heel after one of these (5)
4 There's an air of missed opportunity (5)
5 You're on the front foot with this one (4)

DOWN

1 Use for hanging pictures (4)
3 This won't be rewarded with a piece of cake (5)

REBUS

A special moment when you achieve this on the course…

ONE
HOLE

RIDDLE

A little help getting around the course is the answer to this riddle.

My first is in slice and also in ace
My second is in eagle but not in bogey
My third is in wood and also in wedge
My fourth is in under but not in over
My fifth is in Tiger and also in drive
My sixth is in green and also in fringe
My seventh is in swing but not in win

What am I?

MISSING VOWELS

There are currently five women's Major tournaments. Since 2010 some players have been multiple winners. Can you find the missing vowels in their names?

NN NRDQVST

RY JTNGRN

BRK HNDRSN

CHN N-G

NB PRK

K JN-YNG

LYDA K

MNJ L

PRK SNG-HYN

RY S-YN

PAIRS GAME

Match up the 20 golfers in 20 seconds. The first one has been done for you.

TRIVIA

In 1971, American Alan Shepard famously played golf away from what would be recognized as a normal course. Where did he play?

a) Summit of Mount Everest

b) Bottom of the Grand Canyon

c) Surface of the Moon

TRIVIA

At the British Open in 1991, Richard Boxall was playing with Colin Montgomerie when his round was suddenly stopped. What had happened?

a) He was attacked by a seagull while eating a banana.

b) His leg snapped while teeing off on the 9th.

c) Monty knocked him out while attempting to swat a wasp with his 5-iron.

WORD SEARCH

ON THE GOLF COURSE

S	D	N	U	O	B	F	O	T	U	O
K	F	H	N	H	T	N	R	M	T	L
C	A	X	G	V	O	E	V	D	D	M
I	I	Y	B	U	K	L	G	R	J	P
T	R	L	N	N	O	T	E	E	T	X
S	W	Y	U	E	X	R	D	T	T	R
G	A	B	R	N	E	J	K	X	J	M
A	Y	P	R	J	J	R	J	Y	M	Z
L	Q	P	U	J	B	X	G	P	M	W
F	N	Y	Q	C	Y	T	X	Q	J	Z

Bunker, Rough, Flagstick, Fairway, Green,
Cup, Tee, Hole, Out Of Bounds

CROSSWORD

CLUB TYPES

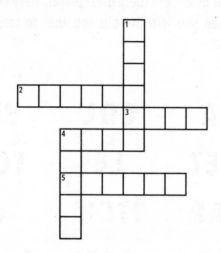

ACROSS

2 Pet rut (anagram) (6)
3 In Scotland it's brewed (4)
4 You can't see it for the trees (4)
5 They will get you there (6)

DOWN

1 Is two things together (6)
4 Use the thick edge, not the thin one (5)

WORD JUMBLE

Some notable golfers made their names as the game for women became firmly established in the twentieth century. The surnames of some of these great players have been jumbled up below. Can you join the bits together to reassemble the eight names?

ZA	COL	WR
WET	LE	TON
HAR	ITCH	BE
HE	LET	IGHT
IAS	BAR	RAW
RED	LS	RG

MAZE

Can you help our golfer putt her way to the flag?

ANAGRAMS
UNDER PAR

Rearrange these letters to reveal four words for those holes achieved under par:

I RID BE

LE AGE

TOSS LA BAR

DR NO CO

TRIVIA

In 1457, Scottish King James II banned the playing of golf. Why did he do this?

a) He was concerned it would affect the archery skills of his troops.

b) Too many cows and sheep were choking on golf balls.

c) It was costing a fortune to replace the broken panes in his palace windows.

WORD LADDER

In this word ladder, change one letter at a time to turn the word PICK into BALL.

PICK
_ _ _ _
_ _ _ _
_ _ _ _
_ _ _ _
BALL

DOT-TO-DOT

Join the dots to find the mystery image.

TRIVIA

In 2021, at the ANA Inspiration, New Zealand golfer Lydia Ko shot the record lowest score in a final round of a women's Major tournament.

What did she sign for?

a) 61

b) 62

c) 63

SPOT THE DIFFERENCE

Can you find the ten differences between these two pictures?

COUNTING CONUNDRUM

🚩🚩 + 🚩🚩 + 🚩🚩 = 48

(🏌️🏌️ x 🚩🚩) + 🚩🚩 = 240

🏆 + (🚩 x 🎒) = 60

🏆🏆 + (🚩 x 🎒🎒) = ?

MISSING VOWELS

Here are the names of the most recent US Masters winners with the vowels deleted. Can you name them in full?

DM SCTT
BBB WTSN
DNNY WLLTT
DSTN JHNSN
HDK MTSYM
JRDN SPTH
PTRCK RD
SCTT SCHFFLR
SRG GRC
TGR WDS

TRIVIA

Legendary actor Sean Connery became a keen golfer after appearing as James Bond in the film Goldfinger. In the movie, 007 is playing against villain Auric Goldfinger. To get his attention, Bond drops an object on the green as Goldfinger is about to putt. What was the object?

a) A pair of pants

b) A bar of Nazi gold

c) A pistol made of gold

REBUS

You might need a drop if your ball has landed in this…

REPAIR
GROUND

ANAGRAMS
ROYAL OCCASIONS

Rearrange these letters to find four Royal courses that are sometimes Open:

NO ROT

ABLE DIRK

OO REV PILL

GG STEREOS

TRIVIA

Golf requires players to follow etiquette and protocol at all times. Before their first shot, a golfer must:

a) address the ball

b) address the Haggis

c) get the home address of their opponent so they can send a thank you note after the game

RIDDLE

A club that features in every bag is the answer to this riddle.

My first is in blade but not in face
My second is in grip but not in yips
My third is in pitch and in lip
My fourth is in divot and not in toed
My fifth is in hosel but not in shaft
My sixth is in draw but not in fade

What am I?

DOT-TO-DOT

Join the dots to find the mystery image.

SPOT THE DIFFERENCE

Can you find the ten differences between these two pictures?

MISSING VOWELS

The most famous golf course in the world is in Fife in Scotland. Can you find the missing vowels to make up these well-known features of the Old Course in St Andrews?

SWLCN BRDG

TH LP

HLL BNKR

RD HL

VLLY F SN

LYSN FLDS

CHP'S BNKR

MSS GRNGR'S BSMS

LD RLWY SHDS

TH SPCTCLS

PAIRS GAME

Match up the 20 golf clubs in 20 seconds. The first one has been done for you.

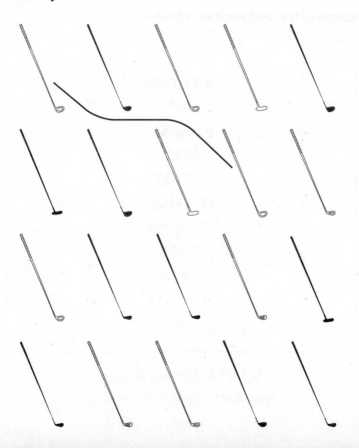

WORD SEARCH

GOLF BALL BRANDS

R	T	A	T	I	T	L	E	I	S	T
C	E	A	B	F	S	N	E	L	L	G
A	D	G	Y	H	J	N	L	O	S	P
L	C	K	N	L	R	I	E	Q	R	I
L	P	M	U	E	O	T	C	S	I	N
A	Z	A	D		Z	R	V	G	X	N
W	I	L	S	O	N	A	M	Y	O	A
A	F	W	I	B	H	N	L	A	N	C
Y	K	O	S	L	X	E	J	S	D	L
B	R	I	D	G	E	S	T	O	N	E

Titleist, TaylorMade, Callaway, Wilson, Pinnacle,
Bridgestone, Srixon, Snell, Slazenger

TRIVIA

Some golfers acquire nicknames – some complimentary, some less so. Which three-time Major winner earned the nickname "The Big Fijian"?

a) Krishna Singh

b) Dinesh Chand

c) Vijay Singh

WORD JUMBLE

Various parts of a golf club have been jumbled up below. Join the bits together to reassemble eight components.

EL	ULE	IP
FA	GR	GR
SO	SH	OOV
HE	CE	LE
EL	ES	HOS
FE	RR	AFT

MAZE

Can you help our golfer choose the best route to the pin?

TRIVIA

The world's longest putt was made in 1999 over the Atlantic. On his way to the Ryder Cup, José María Olazábal putted down the length of Concorde's cabin as the airliner was travelling at twice the speed of sound. How far did the ball travel?

a) 5.5 miles

b) 9.2 miles

c) 21.1 miles

MISSING VOWELS

The US Open tournament is like the British Open in that it rotates around different courses. Some courses have hosted the event more than once. Can you find the missing vowels in their names?

PNHRST

KMNT

SHNNCCK HLLS

PBBL BCH

MRN

KLND HLLS

WNGD FT

BLTSRL

LYMPC CLB

TH CNTRY CLB

WORD LADDER

In this word ladder, change one letter at a time to turn the word CARRY into PUTTS.

| CARRY |
| _ _ _ _ _ |
| _ _ _ _ _ |
| _ _ _ _ _ |
| _ _ _ _ _ |
| PUTTS |

PAIRS GAME

Match up the 20 golfers in 20 seconds. The first one has been done for you.

TRIVIA

Golf has many aphorisms and quotes. One of the most well-known is "Drive for show but putt for dough", meaning the real money is won on the putting green. Which South African player is reputed to have coined the phrase?

a) Gary Player

b) Ernie Els

c) Bobby Locke

WORD WHEEL

From the nine letters below, how many words of four or more letters can you make? All words must include the central letter. Can you find the name of a large feature of all golf courses that uses all the letters?

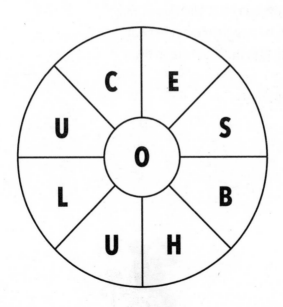

RIDDLE

Something to be avoided is the answer to this riddle.

My first is in blade but not in play
My second is in club but not in ball
My third is in run and also in turn
My fourth is in links and also in sink
My fifth is in eagle but not in plug
My sixth is in drive but not in divot

What am I?

COUNTING CONUNDRUM

x = 72

x = 48

x = 54

= ? = ? = ?

TRIVIA

Before Babe Zaharias began her successful golfing career, she won three medals at the 1932 Olympic Games. What were these three events?

a) Javelin, high jump and 80 m hurdles

b) Shot put, discus and 4 x 100 m relay

c) Fencing, pole vault and triple jump

MISSING VOWELS

Here are the names of some of the best male players who never won a Major with the vowels removed. Can you find the missing letters?

CLN MNTGMR

L WSTWD

PL CSY

LK DNLD

RCK FWLR

N PLTR

JY HS

TT KCHR

PTRCK CNTLY

XNDR SCHFFL

PAIRS GAME

Match up the 20 trophies in 20 seconds. The first one has been done for you.

CROSSWORD

WOMEN'S CAREER GRAND SLAM WINNERS

ACROSS

1 Could be a member of Madness (5)

2 Deserved more than a "pat" on the back for winning 31 tour events (7)

3 Won two Majors in three successive decades (7)

4 Winning 13 Majors was not unlucky for this player (6)

DOWN

1 Perhaps the greatest? (9)

4 From down under, often under par (4)

TRIVIA

At the 1961 Open, Arnold Palmer won by one stroke. This close victory came despite an occurrence on the 16th hole in his second round. What happened?

a) When Palmer's drive went into the spectators, one of them threw it 30 yards towards the green.

b) Palmer's ball moved in a bunker as he was about to play and he called a penalty on himself, despite no one else seeing it.

c) On the green, Palmer tripped and his club knocked his playing partner's ball into the hole.

SPOT THE DIFFERENCE

Can you find the ten differences between these two pictures?

REBUS

It's something you have to do to get the ball in…

SINK_ _ _ _ S

ANAGRAMS
GREAT GOLFERS OF THE 1960s

Rearrange these letters to reveal the surnames of four players from this decade:

ME RALP

AND RESS

LACK JIN

LAME

TRIVIA

American golfer Fred Couples earned a nickname for his power off the tee. What name summed up his prowess with the driver?

a) Boom Boom

b) Fred the Shred

c) The Driving Instructor

RIDDLE

A well-known British female golfer is the answer to this riddle.

My first is in teed and also in tied
My second is in major and also in medal
My third is in drive but not in draw
My fourth is in iron but not in green
My fifth is in range but not in grain
My sixth is in senior but not in iron.

Who am I?

REBUS

You'll need a strong back leg to deal with this…

E
I
L

WORD WHEEL

From the nine letters below, how many words of four or more letters can you make? All words must include the central letter. Using all the letters can you find the name of a British course known for previously hosting the Ryder Cup?

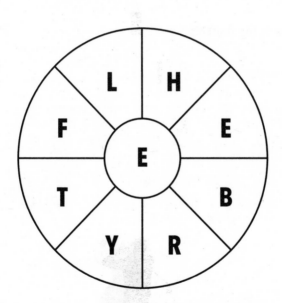

TRIVIA

At the Open in 1977, Jack Nicklaus and Tom Watson competed together on the Sunday for the championship. Their epic last round gained which nickname?

a) Turnberry Tussle

b) Battle of the Bunkers

c) Duel in the Sun

PAIRS GAME

Can you match the most recent Ryder Cups with their courses?
The first one has been done for you.

2021	Valhalla
2018	The K Club
2016	The American Club
2014	Medinah
2012	Le Golf National
2010	The Belfry
2008	Oakland Hills
2006	Hazeltine National
2004	Gleneagles
2002	Celtic Manor

ANAGRAMS
GRAND SLAMS

Rearrange these letters to reveal five male players who have won all four Majors in their careers:

GEEZE SAN RAN

HOG BANEN

IN SLACK CAJUK

SO DO WIT REG

ALP YER YARG

WORD SEARCH

CUP COMPETITIONS

A	C	J	M	E	Q	H	U	O	Y	L
K	M	I	E	H	L	O	S	C	I	L
X	X	B	A	L	P	Y	F	N	K	I
C	S	E	K	P	S	W	R	D	N	H
B	U	Z	D	R	Y	D	E	R	Q	N
W	G	R	P	E	L	R	U	V	I	U
A	J	O	T	S	F	E	Y	C	S	D
L	F	V	Z	I	F	M	R	J	H	D
K	W	B	T	D	S	G	A	X	L	E
E	E	I	S	E	N	H	O	W	E	R
R	A	L	Q	N	C	I	E	N	J	F
F	S	O	X	T	V	P	G	A	P	L
W	D	H	U	S	K	R	M	B	G	A

FedEx, Presidents, Solheim, Ryder, Curtis, Walker,
PGA, Alfred Dunhill, Eisenhower

61

TRIVIA

Golf goes back centuries and has been played by some famous historical figures. In 1567, Mary Queen of Scots was criticized for playing golf just days after an historic event had taken place. What was the event?

a) Her husband Lord Darnley had been murdered.

b) She had just given birth to the future King James.

c) She had written a letter to England's Queen Elizabeth asking if she could be queen instead.

SPOT THE DIFFERENCE

Can you find the ten differences between these two pictures?

REBUS

A golfer can't hit a shot without this…

GNIWS

ANAGRAMS
A LITTLE HELP

Rearrange these letters to reveal four materials used to fill early golf balls:

THE FEARS

CHAP TAG TRUE

RE BRUB

WARTS

TRIVIA

Legendary Spanish golfer Seve Ballesteros won the first of his five Majors at Royal Lytham & St Annes in 1979. On the final round, at the 16th hole, his wayward drive meant he had to play his second shot from where?

a) A child's play park

b) The roof of an ice cream van

c) A car park

MISSING VOWELS

The US Masters tournament is always played at the Augusta National. Each hole on the course is named after a tree or shrub. Can you find the missing vowels to name them?

Hole 1: T LV

Hole 3: FLWRNG PCH

Hole 5: MGNL

Hole 6: JNPR

Hole 7: PMPS

Hole 10: CMLL

Hole 13: ZL

Hole 15: FRTHRN

Hole 16: RDBD

Hole 17: NNDN

COUNTING CONUNDRUM

+ = 15

x = 54

- = 3

= ?   = ?

ANAGRAMS
GREAT GOLFERS OF THE 1970s

Rearrange these letters to reveal the surnames of four male players from this decade:

IN OVERT

IM RELL

OF WE SKIP

WINIR

TRIVIA

In 2008, Inbee Park became the youngest player to win the US Women's Open. How old was she?

a) 18

b) 19

c) 20

WORD JUMBLE

Surnames of male players of the early twentieth century have been jumbled up below. Join the bits together to reassemble eight great players.

NES	GAN	UR
EAD	RA	MO
HO	HA	ON
CO	ZEN	SN
LO	AR	TT
JO	CKE	
GEN	SA	

DOT-TO-DOT

Join the dots to find the mystery image.

CROSSWORD

CLUB TYPES

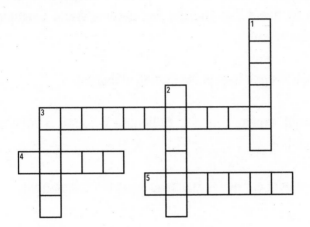

ACROSS

3 Can clean up with this one (11)

4 Only the sharpest can cut with this (5)

5 You need these for walking (4, 3)

DOWN

1 The face behind the front of the shaft (6)

2 Hammering in the birdies or tent pegs (6)

3 Have you the stomach for this putter? (5)

TRIVIA

In 1966, England's men's football team won the World Cup. On the day of the final, Scotland forward Denis Law went golfing. When he heard that England had become World Champions, what did he do?

a) Threw his golf bag on the ground in disgust

b) Bought everyone in the clubhouse a round of drinks to celebrate

c) Went back out on the course to avoid the celebrations

PAIRS GAME

Match up the 20 golf carts in 20 seconds. The first one has been done for you.

WORD LADDER

In this word ladder, change one letter at a time to turn the word TEED into GOLF.

TEED

_ _ _ _

_ _ _ _

_ _ _ _

_ _ _ _

GOLF

RIDDLE

What you get when you go out of bounds is the answer to this riddle.

My first is in play and also in lip
My second is in drive but not in iron
My third is in fringe and also in green
My fourth is in hazard and also in draw
My fifth is in hole and also in glove
My sixth is in pitch but not in chip
My seventh is in caddy but not in card

What am I?

TRIVIA

Harry Vardon, James Braid and J. H. Taylor dominated the men's game in the late nineteenth and early twentieth centuries. They were known collectively as:

a) The Great Britons

b) The Great Lads

c) The Great Triumvirate

WORD WHEEL

See how many words of four or more letters you can make from the letters below, making sure to include the central letter. Can you find where the British Open was first played using all the letters?

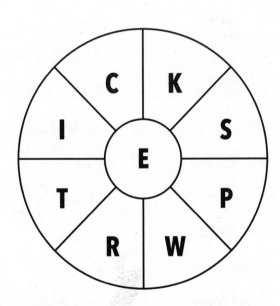

PAIRS GAME

Can you match the ten players with their nicknames? The first one has been done for you.

Greg Norman	The Black Knight
Ernie Els	Big Wiesy
Gary Player	Great White Shark
Annika Sörenstam	Peacock of the Fairways
Craig Stadler	The Mechanic
Doug Sanders	Wild Thing
Michelle Wie West	Mrs 59
Miguel Ángel Jiménez	Chippie
John Daly	The Walrus
Paul Lawrie	The Big Easy

COUNTING CONUNDRUM

+ + = 15

(x) + = 35

+ (x) = 100

+ (x) = ?

TRIVIA

There are four men's Major tournaments:

- US Open
- Masters
- US PGA
- British Open

Can you place the championships in chronological order of when they were first held?

1860 _____

1895 _____

1916 _____

1934 _____

ANAGRAMS
GREAT GOLFERS OF THE 1980s

Rearrange these letters to reveal the surnames of four male players from this decade:

LEN RAG

SELL SORE BAT

SAW MOON

DO FLY

DOT-TO-DOT

Join the dots to find the mystery image.

WORD LADDER

In this word ladder, change one letter at a time to turn the word
TEES into HOLE.

TEES

_ _ _ _

_ _ _ _

_ _ _ _

_ _ _ _

HOLE

TRIVIA

American Mickey Wright is regarded as one of the best women golfers of all time. She won many tournaments in the USA but didn't travel much abroad. Why was this?

a) Her passport had lapsed and she was too busy to get it updated.

b) Wright was not a good flyer and avoided air travel where possible.

c) She missed her pets too much when away.

WORD JUMBLE

Golfers can play several different types of game. Can you reassemble eight formats from the parts below?

ST	ST	AB	AP	AMB
BE	UR	UR	CHP	CH
FO	FO	SO	ST	MAT
LE	FO	SCR	ROK	MAN
LL	LL	LAY	LAY	LE
RD	BA	BA	EP	ME

SPOT THE DIFFERENCE

Can you find the ten differences between these two pictures?

COUNTING CONUNDRUM

+ = 13

+ = 12

+ = 11

= ?   = ?   = ?

TRIVIA

Every year at the US Masters the previous year's winner gets to choose the menu for the Champions' Dinner. Following Tiger Woods' win in 1997, what food did the 22-year-old select?

a) Cheeseburger, apple pie and ice cream, milkshake

b) Pizza, banana split, slushy

c) Chicken goujons, cupcakes, blackcurrant squash

PAIRS GAME

Match the 20 golfers in 20 seconds. The first one has been done for you.

WORD WHEEL

See how many words of four or more letters you can make from the letters below. All words must include the central letter. Using all the letters, can you find the name of something on the course everyone aims at?

WORD SEARCH

WELL-KNOWN CADDIES

E	V	O	R	G	S	U	M	B	D	F
A	G	C	M	K	I	S	O	L	N	S
W	R	P	U	S	M	T	A	V	Q	U
Y	I	J	W	A	D	R	X	H	N	N
A	E	L	C	I	E	E	C	L	A	E
G	N	K	L	G	T	B	H	M	W	S
R	A	P	Z	I	Z	O		Q	O	S
Y	L	T		F	A	R	J	B	C	O
N	I	L	D	E	M	M	O	T	V	N
F	S	F	Y	L	E	S	S	U	K	W

Sunesson, Williams, Mackay, Fyles, Musgrove,
Fitzgerald, Roberts, Medlin, Cowan

TRIVIA

The first rules of golf were written down by a society established in Edinburgh in 1744. What was this society called?

a) The Gentlemen Golfers of Leith

b) The Mashie Niblick Men of Morningside

c) The Polite Players of Portobello

DOT-TO-DOT

Join the dots to find the mystery image.

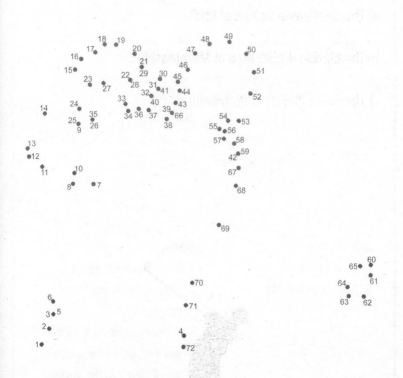

CROSSWORD

THINGS YOU CAN DO TO A PUTT

ACROSS
3 Give up (7)
5 Not Ms or Mrs (4)

DOWN
1 Can you create one? (4)
2 There's 18 of these on a course (4)
4 A thirsty golfer will do this to a pint at the 19th hole (5)
6 You'll find it in the kitchen (4)

PAIRS GAME

Match up the 20 golf courses in 20 seconds. The first one has been done for you.

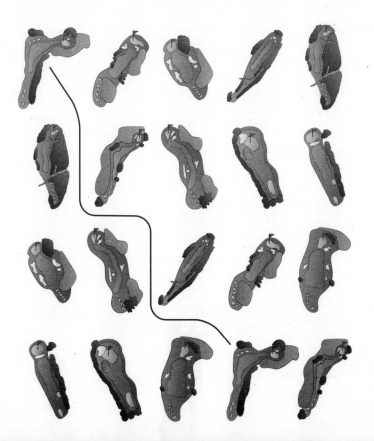

TRIVIA

Following his team's victory at the 2018 Ryder Cup, European captain Thomas Bjørn fulfilled a promise and had a part of his body tattooed with the winning score: 17½ – 10½. Which body part was it?

a) His leg

b) His ankle

c) His buttocks

WORD SEARCH

CLUB SHAFT MATERIAL

E	S	A	C	G	M	J	E	M	V	H
T	A	S	H	P	B	O	U	D	H	X
I	N	T	A	K	R	I	T	A	I	F
H	S	E	U	L	N	L	Z	Q	C	I
P	Z	E	W	A	G	E	C	A	K	Y
A	F	L	T	I	L	E	L	J	O	R
R	B	I	G	D	S	U	R	F	R	M
G	T	N	Q	P	K	X	E	B	Y	D
M	U	I	N	I	M	U	L	A	I	V
T	H	B	O	R	O	N	Y	W	O	F

Titanium, Ash, Hazel, Boron, Hickory,
Fibreglass, Aluminium, Steel, Graphite

REBUS

A handy technique for approach shots.

E SWING

ANAGRAMS
GREAT GOLFERS OF THE 1990s

Rearrange these letters to reveal the surnames of four male players from this decade:

DO LAF

TEST WAR

ALLA OZ BA

MAO ERA

TRIVIA

Jack Nicklaus is one of the game's greatest ever players. His tally of 18 Majors remains the highest for any player. His nickname is:

a) Golden Bear

b) Fozzie Bear

c) Jack Frost

MAZE

Can you help our golfer get to the flag?

WORD JUMBLE

Eight things you would find on a golf course have been jumbled up below. Can you join the bits together to reassemble the eight different things?

GR	BUN	TEE
IR	KER	UGH
WAY	HAZ	FR
EEN	OU	BOU
RO	ARD	IN
FA	ER	GE
TOF	WAT	NDS

WORD SEARCH

OLD CLUBS

K	E	E	L	C	N	E	D	O	O	W
A	C	I	K	M	O	Q	S	B	Y	E
T	M	A	S	H	I	E	U	E	D	R
J	F	B	K	C	I	L	B	I	N	E
I	N	J	R	L	C	H	P	F	G	T
G	V	O	O	Y	A	D	X	F	U	F
G	B	R	A	S	S	I	E	A	B	O
E	B	L	F	J	H	W	K	B	G	L
R	P	A	I	N	O	O	P	S	U	C
S	X	L	D	T	K	M	Y	P	B	Q

Play Club, Brassie, Spoon, Baffie, Mashie,
Niblick, Wooden Cleek, Lofter, Jigger

105

PAIRS GAME

Match up the 20 vintage golfers in 20 seconds. The first one has been done for you.

MISSING VOWELS

With its human stories and dramatic moments, golf is an ideal subject for movies. Can you find the missing vowels to name these ten golfing films?

CDDYSHCK

TN CP

TMMY'S HNR

TH PHNTM F TH PN

HPPY GLMR

TH LGND F BGGR VNC

TH GRTST GM VR PLYD

TH CDDY

DD SLD PRFCT

SVN DYS N TP

COUNTING CONUNDRUM

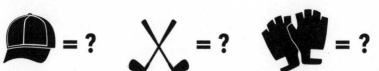

🧢 + 🧢 = 22

⛳ x 🧤 = 156

⛳ + 🧢 = 24

🧢 = ?   ⛳ = ?   🧤 = ?

DOT-TO-DOT

Join the dots to find the mystery image.

TRIVIA

Harry Vardon is one of the game's greatest players, who famously won six Opens – a record that still stands. He gave his name to a type of grip, but what is it also known as?

a) Overlapping

b) Interlocking

c) Baseball

WORD WHEEL

See how many words of four or more letters you can make from the letters below. All words must include the central letter. Can you find the item that golfers need to keep a record of their round?

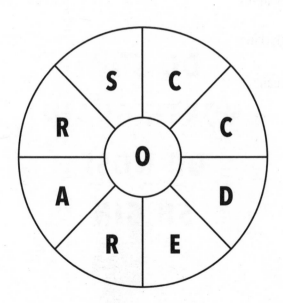

ANAGRAMS
GREAT GOLFERS OF THE 2000s

Rearrange these letters to reveal the surnames of four male players from this decade:

DO SOW

NORTH GRAIN

GO NOSE

SH GIN

REBUS

You'll have to take a turn at this…

SUMS

SUMS

SUMS

SUMS

TRIVIA

A bump-and-run is:

a) when golf carts collide on the fairway

b) a way of playing on windy links courses

c) when a player's ball cannons into an opponent's on the green

SPOT THE DIFFERENCE

Can you find the ten differences between these two pictures?

BETWEEN THE LINES

Reading downwards, nine three-letter words can be made that when all in place will form the name of a Scottish championship course in the blank line. Can you name that course?

I	R	S	C	O	W	P	A	O
P	N	T	Y	F	T	G	L	E

REBUS

Sporting apparel not seen as often as in the past...

+4

+4

+4

+4

WORD SEARCH

FINAL DAY MAJOR COLLAPSES

V	B	E	H	S	J	C	G	M	U	I
K	A	L	D	A	S	P	I	E	T	H
O	M	N	R	N	M	C	F	Q	N	N
T	C	S	D	D	K	P	V	O	C	A
E	I	F	W	E	G	N	S	D	H	M
M	L	T	L	R	V	N	K	O	I	R
J	R	S	T	S	H	E	R	Y	T	O
U	O	W	L	O	V	M	L	B	E	N
N	Y	A	J	F	C	H	P	D	G	X
S	C	Q	R	Z	N	S	N	E	E	D

Sanders, Norman, Scott, Van de Velde, Mickelson,
Spieth, McIlroy, Sneed, Johnson

118

COUNTING CONUNDRUM

+ + + = 64

+ (+) = 72

- = 8

+ (x) = ?

RIDDLE

A shot that the other players agree can count automatically without being played is the answer to this riddle.

My first is in Tiger and also in Greg
My second is in Trevino but not Poulter
My third is in O'Meara and also in Rahm
My fourth is in Palmer but not in Player
My fifth is in Ballesteros and also in Stewart

WORD WHEEL

See how many words of four or more letters you can make from the letters below. All words must include the central letter. Can you find this Scandinavian superstar?

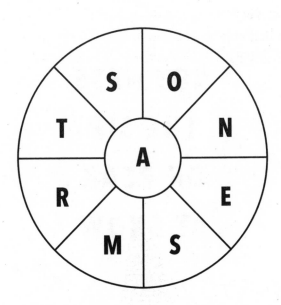

ANAGRAMS
GREAT GOLFERS OF THE 2010s

Rearrange these letters to reveal the surnames of four male players from this decade:

NOT NESS

THE SIP

OK PEAK

AT SNOW

WORD LADDER

In this word ladder, change one letter at a time to turn PUSH into HOOK.

PUSH
_ _ _ _
_ _ _ _
_ _ _ _
_ _ _ _
HOOK

TRIVIA

Nominative determinism is when a person's name reflects the job they do. Which of the following is NOT a real golfer?

a) Danielle Masters

b) Tammie Green

c) Lonnie Bunker

REBUS

A special moment when you achieve this on the championship course…

CLU**LEADER**USE

TRIVIA

Golfer Gloria Minoprio received criticism and a place in the history books for what she did at the English Women's Golf Championship at Westward Ho! in October 1933. Which of the following are true about her participation in that event?

a) She was the first woman to wear trousers in a golf tournament

b) She used only one club throughout: a "cleek" (2-iron)

c) She was late to the tee and almost forfeited her match before arriving in a chauffeur-driven Rolls-Royce

CROSSWORD

ELEMENTS OF A SWING

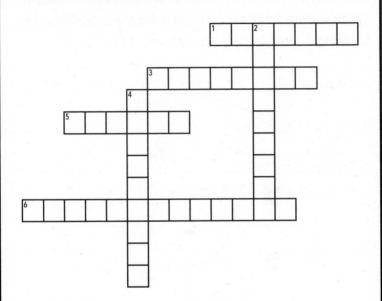

ACROSS
1 The beginning has to be first-class (7)
3 For those hungry in a hurry (8)
5 Sudden… (6)
6 After it's on its way (6,7)

DOWN
2 Not going up (9)
4 Going up (9)

WORD WHEEL

See how many words of four or more letters you can make from the letters below. All words must include the central letter. Can you find the name of a male, six-time Major winner that uses all the letters?

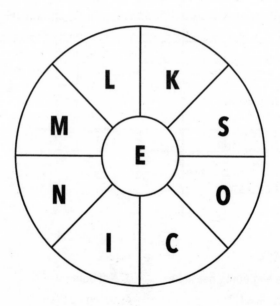

TRIVIA

The 1969 Ryder Cup came down to the final hole in the final match between the Briton Tony Jacklin and the American Jack Nicklaus. They reached the 18th green even, and after Nicklaus putted for his four, he lifted Jacklin's marker, saving his opponent having to make the two-foot putt. This meant the competition was a tie, although America retained the trophy, having won the previous event. This great act of sportsmanship is known as:

a) The Accession

b) The Succession

c) The Concession

PAIRS GAME

Match up the 20 flags in 20 seconds. The first one has been done for you.

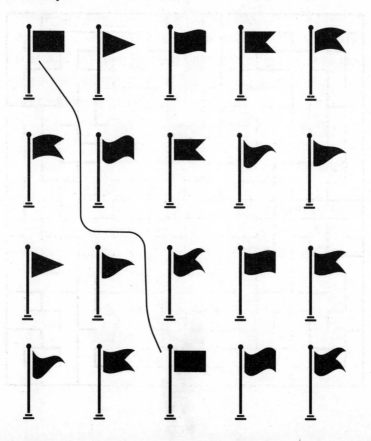

MAZE

Can you help our golfer putt her way to the trophy?

ANSWERS

p.6, Crossword: Bad Shots
Across: 2 top, 3 shank, 4 whiff, 5 toed
Down: 1 hook, 3 slice

p.7, Rebus
A hole in one

p.8, Riddle
Caddies

p.9, Missing Vowels
Anna Nordqvist, Ariya Jutanugarn, Brooke Henderson, Chun In-Gee, Inbee Park, Ko Jin-Young, Lydia Ko, Minjee Lee, Park Sung-Hyun, Ryu So-Yeon

p.10, Pairs Game

p.11, Trivia
c)

p.12, Trivia
b)

p.13, Word Search:
On the Golf Course

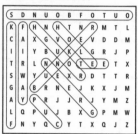

p.14, Crossword: Club Types
Across: 2 putter, 3 iron, 4 wood, 5 driver
Down: 1 hybrid, 4 wedge

p. 15, Word Jumble
Zaharias, Wethered, Collett, Leitch, Barton, Wright, Rawls, Berg

p.16, Maze

p.17, Anagrams: Under Par
Birdie, eagle, albatross, condor

p.18, Trivia
a)

p.19, Word Ladder
One possible solution: pick, sick, silk, sill, bill, ball

p.20, Dot-to-Dot

p.21, Trivia
b)

p.22, Spot the Difference

p.23, Counting Conundrum
flag=8, bag=7, trophy=4.
Sum: 8+(8x14)=120

p.24, Missing Vowels
Adam Scott, Bubba Watson, Danny Willett, Dustin Johnson, Hideki Matsuyama, Jordan Spieth, Patrick Reed, Scottie Scheffler, Sergio García, Tiger Woods

p.25, Trivia
b)

p.26, Rebus
Ground under repair

p.27, Anagrams: Royal Occasions
Troon, Birkdale, Liverpool, St Georges

p.28, Trivia
a)

p.29, Riddle
Driver

p.30, Dot-to-Dot

p.31, Spot the Difference

p.32, Missing Vowels

Swilcan Bridge, The Loop, Hell Bunker, Road Hole, Valley of Sin, Elysian Fields, Cheape's Bunker, Miss Grainger's Bosoms, Old Railway Sheds, The Spectacles

p.33, Pairs Game

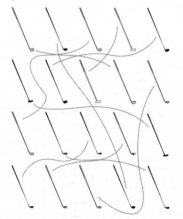

p.34, Word Search: Golf Ball Brands

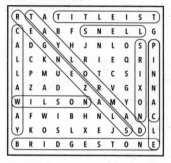

p.35, Trivia
c)

p.36, Word Jumble
Shaft, face, sole, grip, heel, grooves, hosel, ferrule

p.37, Maze

p.38, Trivia
b)

p.39, Missing Vowels
Pinehurst, Oakmont, Shinnecock Hills, Pebble Beach, Merion, Oakland Hills, Winged Foot, Baltusrol, Olympic Club, The Country Club

p.40, Word Ladder
One possible solution: carry, parry, party, patty, putty, putts

p.41, Pairs Game

p.42, Trivia
c)

p.43, Word Wheel
Word that uses all letters = clubhouse

p.44, Riddle
Bunker

p.45, Counting Conundrum
Female golfer=9, male golfer=8, junior golfer=6

p.46, Trivia
a)

p.47, Missing Vowels
Colin Montgomerie, Lee Westwood, Paul Casey, Luke Donald, Rickie Fowler, Ian Poulter, Jay Haas, Matt Kuchar, Patrick Cantlay, Xander Schauffele

p.48, Pairs Game

p.49, Crossword: Women's Career Grand Slam Winners
Across: 1 Suggs, 2 Bradley
3 Inkster, 4 Wright
Down: 1 Sörenstam, 4 Webb

p.50, Trivia
b)

p.51, Spot the Difference

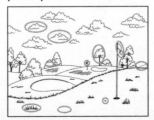

p.52, Rebus
Hole out

p.53, Anagrams: Great Golfers of the 1960s
Palmer, Sanders, Jacklin, Lema

p.54, Trivia
a)

p.55, Riddle
Davies

p.56, Rebus
Uphill lie

p.57, Word Wheel
Words that use all letters = The Belfry

p.58, Trivia
c)

p.59, Pairs Game
2021 - The American Club,
2018 - Le Golf National,
2016 - Hazeltine National,
2014 - Gleneagles,
2012 - Medinah,
2010 - Celtic Manor,
2008 - Valhalla,
2006 - The K Club,
2004 - Oakland Hills,
2002 - The Belfry

p.60, Anagrams: Grand Slams
Gene Sarazen, Ben Hogan, Jack Nicklaus, Tiger Woods, Gary Player

p.61, Word Search: Cup Competitions

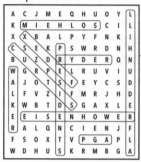

p.62, Trivia
a)

p.63, Spot the Difference

p.64, Rebus
Backswing

p.65, Anagrams: A little help
Feathers, gutta percha, rubber, straw

p.66, Trivia
c)

p.67, Missing Vowels
Hole 1: Tea Olive, Hole 3: Flowering Peach, Hole 5: Magnolia, Hole 6: Juniper, Hole 7: Pampas, Hole 10: Camellia, Hole 13: Azalea, Hole 15: Firethorn, Hole 16: Redbud, Hole 17: Nandina

p.68, Counting Conundrum
Male golfer=9, female golfer=6

p.69, Anagrams: Great Golfers of the 1970s
Trevino, Miller, Weiskopf, Irwin

p.70, Trivia
b)

p.71, Word Jumble
Hogan, Cotton, Snead, Locke, Jones, Hagen, Sarazen, Armour

p.72, Dot-to-Dot

p.73 Crossword: Club Types
Across: 3 broomhandle, 4 blade, 5 heeltoe
Down: 1 offset, 2 mallet, 3 belly

p.74, Trivia
a)

p.75, Pairs Game

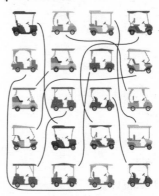

p.76, Word Ladder
One possible solution: teed, weed, weld, geld, gold, golf

p.77, Riddle
Penalty

p.78, Trivia
c)

p.79, Word Wheel
Word that uses all letters = Prestwick

p.80, Pairs Game
Greg Norman - *Great White Shark*, Ernie Els - *The Big Easy*, Gary Player - *The Black Knight*, Annika Sörenstam - *Mrs 59*,

Craig Stadler - *The Walrus*,
Doug Sanders - *Peacock of the Fairways*,
Michelle Wie West - *Big Wiesy*,
Miguel Ángel Jiménez - *The Mechanic*,
John Daly - *Wild Thing*,
Paul Lawrie - *Chippie*

p.81, Counting Conundrum
teed ball=5, iron=10,
wood and ball=9.
Sum: (10)+(9x5)=55

p.82, Trivia
1860 - British Open, 1895 - US Open, 1916 - US PGA, 1934 - Masters

p.83, Anagrams: Great Golfers of the 1980s
Langer, Ballesteros, Woosnam, Floyd

p.84, Dot-to-Dot

p.85, Word Ladder
One possible solution: tees, toes, hoes, hops, hope, hole

p.86, Trivia
b)

p.87, Word Jumble
Stroke play, match play, scramble, Chapman, foursome, four-ball, best ball, Stableford

p.88, Spot the Difference

p.89, Counting Conundrum
buggy=7, club and ball=6, golf ball=5

p.90, Trivia
a)

p.91, Pairs Game

p.92, Word Wheel
Word that uses all letters = flagstick

p.93, Word Search: Well-known Caddies

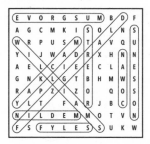

p.94, Trivia
a)

p.95, Dot-to-Dot

p.96, Crossword: Things You Can Do To a Putt
Across: 3 concede, 5 miss
Down: 1 make, 2 hole, 3 drain, 6 sink

p.97, Pairs Game

p.98, Trivia
c)

p.99, Word Search: Club Shaft Material

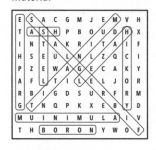

p.100, Rebus
Three-quarter swing

p.101, Anagrams: Great Golfers of the 1990s
Faldo, Stewart, Olazabal, O'Meara

p.102, Trivia
a)

p.103, Maze

p.104, Word Jumble
Green, fairway, bunker, rough, water hazard, tee, fringe, out of bounds

p.105, Word Search: Old Clubs

p.106, Pairs Game

p.107, Missing Vowels
Caddyshack, Tin Cup, Tommy's Honour, The Phantom Of The Open, Happy Gilmore, The Legend Of Bagger Vance, The Greatest Game Ever Played, The Caddy, Dead Solid Perfect, Seven Days In Utopia

p.108, Counting Conundrum
hat=11, crossed clubs=13, gloves=12

p.109, Dot-to-Dot

p.110, Trivia
a)

p.111, Word Wheel
Word that uses all letters = scorecard

p.112, Anagrams: Great Golfers of the 2000s
Woods, Harrington, Goosen, Singh

p.113, Rebus
Foursomes

p.114, Trivia
b)

p.115, Spot the Difference

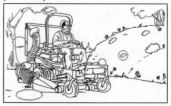

p.116, Between the Lines
Muirfield

p.117, Rebus
Plus fours

p.118, Word Search: Final Day Major Collapses

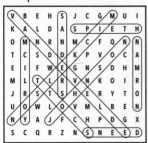

p.119, Counting Conundrum
wood=16, iron=14, ball trophy=11.
Sum: 16+(11x14)=170

p.120, Riddle
Gimme

p.121, Word Wheel
Word that uses all letters = Sorenstam

p.122, Anagrams: Great Golfers of the 2010s
Stenson, Spieth, Koepka, Watson

p.123, Word Ladder
One possible solution: push, posh, pooh, poop, hoop, hook

p.124, Trivia
c)

p.125, Rebus
Leader in the clubhouse

p.126, Trivia
a), b) and c)

p.127, Crossword: Elements of a Swing
Across: 1 address, 3 takeaway, 5 impact, 6 follow through
Down: 2 downswing, 4 backswing

p.128, Word Wheel
Word that uses all letters = Mickelson

p.129, Trivia
c)

p.130, Pairs Game

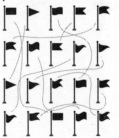

p.131, Maze

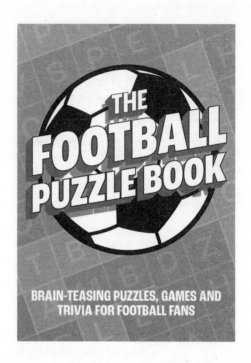

The Football Puzzle Book

Paperback

978-1-80007-921-2

Discover word searches, riddles, crosswords, spot-the-differences
and much more in this fun-filled activity book for football lovers.
Whether you're diving through a maze to make an incredible
save or trying to match the pairs of football boots, this book
is guaranteed to be a favourite for all who enjoy the game.

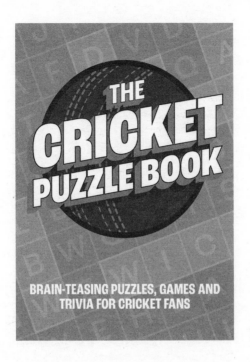

The Cricket Puzzle Book

Paperback

978-1-80007-923-6

Discover word searches, riddles, crosswords, spot-the-differences and much more in this fun-filled activity book for cricket lovers. Whether you're trying to match the pairs of batting gloves or discovering the longest and shortest test matches ever, this book is guaranteed to be a favourite for all who enjoy the game.

Have you enjoyed this book?

If so, find us on Facebook at
Summersdale Publishers, on Twitter at
@Summersdale and on Instagram and TikTok at
@summersdalebooks and get in touch.

We'd love to hear from you!

www.summersdale.com

Image credits